Suicide Monologues

For Actors and Others

Jim Chevallier

Chez Jim Books • North Hollywood, CA

ISBN: 978-0-578-02043-3

Published by:
Chez Jim Books

FOR THE SURVIVORS

These monologues may be used individually for class, audition or production. *Suicide Monologues* may also be produced as a single work, and the order in which the pieces appear is meant to suggest one possible flow for such a production.

Though these monologues have been primarily written to be used by actors, it will be gratifying if others who find their experiences reflected here also make use of them, in whatever context and to whatever degree.

Table of Contents

Stop

The Voice

Why keep hanging around? No one wants you here. You'd be doing the world a service. Doing something useful for once.

Why bother to go on? Why keep trying to find a reason? Why keep convincing yourself that things aren't that bad?

They are, you know, and they're only going to get worse.

Look at you, trying all those tricks: the pills, the therapy, the "positive thoughts". It's pitiful to watch. Depressing, if you want to know. So depressing to watch you.

Why don't you just be done with it? Stop annoying us all. It's so unseemly, I can't tell you. It's such a sickening spectacle.

Stop it, won't you? Just be done with it. Take yourself out of the picture, and let the world move on.

The Life of the Party

I was the life of the party. Even when there was no party. I made one happen. I made people laugh. I made myself laugh.

I worked good and hard to make myself laugh. Lord, you could hear my laugh from a block away.

"Isn't he something, that Lester?" people would say. "Always happy. Look at him. Always with the smile."

Hell, even I thought I was happy. As long as I wasn't alone. I can't tell you how I hated that, being alone.

Oh, not everyone signed on. Sometimes I'd see people frown, or move to another table. Once I heard someone say, "God, I wish that jerk would keep it down." But who cares, right? Party-poopers. You get 'em in every crowd.

Still, it wore me out sometimes, working like that, keeping the motor running, the horn honking, the smoke pouring out. Sometimes I just wanted to come to rest, you know? Stop. Like a shark.

Oh, that's right. Sharks don't stop. They can't. Or they'll die.

So today, I made a mistake. I stayed alone. And then I decided, that's what I'll do. I'll stop. I'll rest.

Oh yeah, and I took some pills. A lot of pills.

Any moment now.

Do you know? I feel great.

Just one thing. Please?

Don't laugh.

Thank You Note

Before I write another word, I must tell you: last night, you outdid yourself. The décor, as always, was superb; all those pastels, the pink and white roses. And that string quartet. However did you get them to come? They haven't played together for years. Or so I'm told. I don't follow such things these days. But your guests were suitably impressed. And, as always, suitably impressive. That Arab ambassador, the prince, insisted I go out on his yacht. It was very kind. I told him I'd love to. That I'd call him next week.

But I was lying.

I was lying because, dear friend, I'm done with next week. I'm done with tomorrow. Soon after I sign this, I'll be done with today.

I can't. I don't how how to say it more plainly than that. "Can't what, my darling?" I hear you say, and for a moment the warmth returns, the eagerness... but it fades. Even – how well I've hid this – even sometimes when I'm with you, it fades.

Columbus was wrong, you know: the world is flat. If you live long enough, and do enough wonderful things, and have enough money, but no purpose, never ever a purpose, it doesn't matter how many flights, how many cruises, how many jaunts you take. How many good causes you lend your name to. Bless me, it wouldn't matter if you took a string and wrapped it around the globe and stood with one end in each hand, you'd still have to accept it, the awful, unfashionable truth: the Earth is flat. There's nothing left to break the monotony, to suggest a sparkle beyond the horizon.

Yes, my dear, the Earth is flat. But I'm about to put a dent in it.

Goodbye, my heart. You almost made Life worth living. Please believe me, it's no fault of yours if you failed.

Stop

I just wanted it to stop.

You couldn't hear it, could you? You thought I was fine.

But I wasn't. It kept getting louder and louder, no matter what I did. No matter how much I blocked it out.

I did everything. I drank, I drugged, I slept around. Nothing worked.

It's easy to say, "You should have held on. You should have been stronger." You didn't hear it. No one did. They heard music, talking. Birds singing. Different sounds. Good sounds.

Me, I only heard one thing. And it just kept getting louder.

Imagine a train coming right at you. Thunder. A hurricane. Your own personal hurricane. Imagine ten times that. And you still wouldn't have it. It still wouldn't be as bad.

And it never stopped. Never. No matter what I did. No matter how much I tried to stop up my ears. It was always there all the time.

Until I did what I did.

You don't see. You think I was weak. That there was another way.

I'm telling you: there wasn't.

All I wanted was for it to stop.

Hurt Someone

He always wanted to hurt someone. That's what it felt like. Even when he laughed, there was something mean in it.

The amazing thing is, people liked him. He got to them somehow. Like they thought, given time, he'd grow out of it. Out of all that anger.

Only, he was forty. Not a kid. He'd had his time, his time to get over it. And he hadn't. Not at all. He'd cuddled up pretty close to it, if you ask me. But he did have that trick. That trick of seeming like he was basically a sweet guy, a guy who'd had some bad breaks.

So people made allowances.

"You're pretty angry," I told him once, and he gave me this little grin. "Yeah, I guess I should work on that." But that was just his way of not working on it. Of saying he'd get around to it. Like a smoker, you know? "I know I should quit," they say, as they light up the next one.

Mostly, no one worried about it. But I did. I worried a lot. I worried he'd hurt someone. Hurt them bad. Maybe even kill them.

I just never figured, it never even crossed my mind, that when it finally happened, when the time came, that the person he would hurt would be himself.

Almost Doesn't Count

Ah yes. The pistol. Properly placed, it opens the back of the head, or puts a bullet neatly through your heart. You might factor in, however, the shaking of your hand, lack of practice or just plain poor aim, in which case, alternate outcomes occur: severing the spinal chord, for instance. The result of this would not be good, but it would not be death, either. And there you'd have gone and done it. Made yourself a burden to your friends.

Oh, I'm sorry. You don't have any friends, do you? Or family. Not in your own mind at least. Not right now. They don't factor in.

Say society, then. You'd become a burden to society.

You could take poison. That works well. Sometimes. When you don't vomit it up, or end your days gasping in awful pain.

How about the subway? A quick leap off the platform, just as the train arrives... No point in telling you about the conductor. Poor bastard will see your face, again and again. Whether or not you succeed. Which you might not want to count on. One woman messed herself up so badly, the next time she tried, she had to roll her wheelchair to the edge. And failed again. Not much left this time. But just enough to keep alive.

'Cause they will, you know. They'll keep you alive. They'll feel obliged. God forbid they should finish the job. They'll do everything they can. And there you'll be, as helpless as a rug. A really ugly, ripped up rug.

Honestly: sound like something worth checking out? Sound like something you're – excuse the expression – dying to try?

White Wine

One day we decided enough was enough. Or maybe she decided. I was past decisions by then. And stone broke. We'd both stopped working months ago. "Let's be done with this," she said. She had some pills she'd saved up. And we had some wine. Cheap white wine.

"Do you want to write a note?" she asked. "No," I said, "Why bother?" We each took a handful of pills, and washed them down with the wine. Then we sat back on the couch, and waited.

I woke up retching. Just puking my guts out. I figured the same thing must have happened to her. Only it hadn't. Nope.

She'd made it. She'd gone all the way.

When I called EMS, they brought the cops too. I got locked up for a little bit.

It's all worked out. I found another job, paid off all my debts. I'm fine now – positive attitude and all. What I figured out is, I was never that badly off. I was only unhappy because of her. So now, yeah, I'm good.

Except for one thing: I can't stand white wine.

Steady

Everybody in the building's been nice. They keep saying how glad they are to see me back at the front desk. And I'm doing rounds again. But only inside.

I'm not ready for outside.

Yesterday, I tried it. Walking around the building. When I got near that spot, my heart started beating. I kept flashing on that blur, whizzing past my eyes. And waiting for the thump...

I rushed back inside.

She could have killed me. She landed that close. But I didn't even think of that, not at the time. Not with the rest of it.

Yesterday my boss saw that look on my face, and he came right over. "You'll make it," he said, "You've always been my best guard. Steady. Steady, and quick with a smile. If anyone can get past this, you can."

I tried to hold on to his words, to how he was trying to help me. But I kept seeing that girl on the sidewalk, with her eye hanging off her face...

It's just, it's gonna take a while, you know?

Red Ropes

If you're watching this on the evening news, the first thing I want you to know is, I didn't do this to get to Heaven. Least of all a Heaven filled with virgins.

I've been with a virgin or two, and let me tell you: not a good time.

Another thing I want to make clear is, I wasn't born poor. No way was I one of the oppressed. In fact, I was a spoiled little....

Oops. Never mind. Got to keep this media-friendly, you know?

Let's put it this way: I lived to party. Red ropes gave way at my step. Skinny blonde heiresses did things with me in back rooms... Well, the kind of things skinny blonde heiresses do on video these days.

Ever think about that? That that's what you've come to? Watching the upper crust go down, and calling that entertainment? Hell, I never thought about it. Not for the longest time. Life was good. I'd been born on the right side of the curve.

Then one day – I was coming off a high, to tell you the truth – I saw this kid in the news. He looked exactly like me. Except he, he was dirt poor. Didn't have a cent. But he'd just won some kind of scholarship. And he looked proud. Like he'd really accomplished something. Like he'd finally got his grip on that first rung. And that was something I'd never been. Proud. Proud of improving on Nature, on whatever blind luck had made me.

That started me on a downward slide. Doors closed, lights out. TV blaring day and night. Not a party in sight. And the lower I sank, the more I wondered: what could I do that would make a difference? What could I do that would show the world how little all that meant to me now: getting into the best clubs, being seen with the best crowd?

Here's where it helped to be watching the news. You see this kind of thing all the time, right? But in some distant dusty land. In one of those places where disaster is standard fare.

Not in the safest, most glamorous places in a great city, where pampered people go to play.

After that, it was a no-brainer. God knows I had the money to buy what I needed. Legally or otherwise.

So tonight, I'm going out again. Won't they be glad to see me after so long? The red ropes will click open, and I'll prance right past the crowd, the crowd of nobodies kept waiting outside.

Lucky for them. Because tonight? Tonight, I'm going clubbing, for the very last time.

Angel

My daughter was killed by an angel. An angel who fell from a church. A girl her own age. A girl who didn't want to live. So she climbed to the top of the church, step by step through one of those old towers, up those winding stairs, and came out, ignoring the tourists and the view – that beautiful view of the city –, walked to the edge, leaned over, and flew.

Did she think she was going to Heaven? Maybe she did. Maybe she thought it was that easy: push free of the gargoyles and the saints, and launch out into the air. Who cares what happens after that?

Who cares where you land?

My daughter wanted to live. With all her heart. She wanted to see the world. That's why she was there – to see the old towers, to see the stained glass. Did she see the girl coming down? Did she look up and think, "Why that must be an angel. Why else would she be in the sky? But the poor thing" – she would have thought that, she would have been concerned – "the poor thing, she's not going to make it. She's starting to fall."

But who expects an angel to fall? Who expects one to come down, headed straight towards you? Did she think, as she saw the girl coming closer, as she almost made out her face, "Oh no, this is my angel, my Angel of Death"? Or did she suddenly see it so clearly at the end, and think, "Oh you fool, you stupid, stupid girl, so what if you didn't want your own life, couldn't you have left me mine?"

Barge

My uncle had a barge, a barge he'd done up inside with varnished wood and brass fittings. It looked like a rich man lived there, instead of my uncle, who barely got by and had a hard face from all his drinking, and lived there alone because no woman could stand him for long, and his nearest neighbors were all scattered farther down the river, and that's why no one could hear me scream when he raped me the day I turned twenty.

My sister usually came along but she'd stopped doing that like she stopped doing everything else and so I had to go see him by myself, which always made me uncomfortable, but he was all the family we had left, and you want to have someone, so sometimes you take what you can get.

I don't remember my father, he left when I was little, and when I think of my mother, I see her face, as red as her brother's, but not from drinking, from screaming and crying, from giving way to whatever kept rising up inside her, until the day it finally burst out and carried her away, away from us, her two little girls. I don't know what poison was in her that that got into my sister too, but in her it was hot, a boiling tide, while in my sister it grew thick and stifling, and slowed her until at last she only had the energy to go out to the woods and use the gun she'd managed to get, and that only leaves me now, and the wonder don't you think isn't that she killed herself, no, the real mystery is why oh why am I still alive?

Midway Down

Midway down, I changed my mind.

The bridge was above me, the water below, and suddenly I saw it: Life hadn't been that bad. Sure, I had a ton of debts, no love life and a long list of aches and pains.

Jumping off a bridge had made perfect sense.

Until I did it. Now it seemed, well... stupid. I had a life – a whole LIFE, dammit – beyond all that stuff and I'd just thrown it away.

Here I was, about to die, and all I could think was: "What a jerk. What a jerk you are."

That really sucked.

And I hit the water.

Only, I didn't die. It turns out you *can* survive jumping off a bridge. (I probably should have looked into that before I did it.) And I did. I survived. Which, basically, felt great. Except for the pain. I thought I hurt before... Now I'd broken both my legs, as well as some ribs, two of which tore up my insides.

Now that, that was pain.

Sure they gave me drugs. Even hooked me up with my own control. But the doctor warned me: "Too much of that stuff, and you'll get hooked." So I dialed it down. Way down.

Because I'd just gotten my life back, and I didn't want to spend it fighting a Jones.

On top of which, the way I see it, if you're going to throw your life away, and then get it back, there's got to be a re-entry fee. And that was mine. Every minute of that month of pain was me, paying my way back in. Paying the price of my return ticket.

I'm here to tell you: it was worth every dime.

14

One Shot

Gun Chant

Pretty, pretty gun. Pretty, pretty glittering gun. Pretty little shiny toy. Shiny, shiny trinket. Pleasing little object. Shiny metal object. Turn it and turn it and turn it around. Watch it sparkle. Watch it glitter. Watch it wink.

Wink-wink.

Look it straight in the eye. Go on, I dare you. Take a good look right up close. Stare deep down into its little soul. Steer your mind into its hollow. Into its distance.

All it takes is an instant. Instantly. Instantly free. Free. Fried. Froth. Froth blown away. Like the foam on the top of your coffee. A wisp of cotton candy.

That easy. That light. That little a loss. Let it go. Let it float. Who could notice? Who could care? Caress. Caress the moment. Only a moment. How little it takes.

Only a moment. How little it takes.....

Truck

You'd think we'd be used to it. But most of the time it's not so bad. People hang themselves, they turn on the gas. If you get them soon enough, it's bearable. Even later, when you get the smell and rot, the maggots, it's not the same.

This one shot himself in his truck. Good-looking guy. He didn't put the barrel in his mouth. Guess he wanted to spare that face. Which was a mercy. But what he did do was aim up from the side, right through the liver towards the heart. Like he wanted to hit a line of vital organs. What a mess. He might as well have split himself open.

We had to be extra careful moving him. Getting him into the bag, torn up like he was, let me tell you, that was no picnic. I thought I saw something dark slip out, into the blood on the floor. But I have to admit, I didn't check.

After that, we washed it down. But only a quick spray. Because it wasn't something we wanted to drag out. We left the truck for his sons to pick up.

I'm still wondering, though, what slid out into all that blood. And if his sons found it later.

If they found a piece of their father in that truck.

Share Your Pain

You don't have to lie to me. Everybody knows he shot himself.

I wish you could hear what they're saying: that he didn't seem like the type; that he must have been drunk. He did like his liquor, didn't he? Oh I know you tried to hide it. Everybody knew. Always making excuses, always trying to cover. But people see through that, you know. People have eyes.

That must be a relief, no? Not having to hide? Aren't you glad to be done with that? Oh my God, don't get me wrong. I'm not saying you're glad he's dead. Who could ever think a thing like that? Still some parts, some parts of it have to be a load off. No?

Anyway, what I wanted to ask, what some of us were wondering is, when is the funeral? Will you have a closed casket? I guess you'll have to, won't you?

Oh God, I'm sorry. That was really insensitive, wasn't it? But if you could just let me know. There's a bunch of us who want to be there.

We really want to be there to share your pain.

Selfish

How could he do that to me? I can't even go down to the store. They'll all be looking at me, talking behind my back. Pretending to pity me. Saying I was a bad wife.

How could he humiliate me like this in front of the whole town?

Wasn't it bad enough he owed everybody money? Or that everyone knew he ran around? I tried to hold my head up, to let people know I was above all that. That I'd married beneath myself – which I had, you know. Still, I tried not to embarrass him the way he embarrassed me. I tried to set an example. To let the children know not to be like their father.

I was counting on my children to make me proud.

God knows how they'll turn out now. No one can blame me if they go off track. Not after what their father's done. A selfish S.O.B. right up to the end. Do you think he thought of that before he pulled the trigger? Not for a moment.

Always thinking of himself. Only himself. As for me? Well, just look.

Look what he's done to me.

Target

My dad was mean to me. I don't mean grumpy or unpleasant mean. I mean vicious, targeted, get under your skin mean. The kind of mean that leaves you thinking about it for days. I don't know why, except maybe I was growing into a man at the same time he was growing old. Or maybe he was mad at himself, so down on himself for being a failure that he didn't know how to do anything but be awful to the rest of us, most especially me, and every time he called me an idiot or a fool or looked like he wanted to hit me, that was him telling himself how worthless he was.

Do you think that was it? Do you think that's why he was such a bastard?

You can see, can't you, where I'd get angry, where I'd start to want to hurt him, where I'd just wish so hard, with my fists and my jaw and my gut clenched as hard as they could get, wishing him away, wishing he wasn't there, like if my thoughts were a death ray, he would have been vaporized, just like that, and when it got hardest, just when I thought that I would be the one to explode, he blew himself away, took himself out of the picture, and there I was with all that hatred, too built up to let go of all at once, and then with that heartbreak too, because I needed him, you know, I mean he was my dad, and then on top of that getting angry because he was gone, and all that coming at me and coming out of me, and me left alone, without knowing who I'm supposed to hurt.

Fall

You should have seen her on the high dive. She loved it. She loved launching off into space.

Like a little girl leaping into her father's arms...

Back then, she had no fear. No fear at all.

She doesn't do a thing now. No sports, nothing. If you ask, she'll say she lost interest. Just lost it. Like a child losing a tooth.

She won't say a word about what happened.

She doesn't go out much either. Not that she's a recluse. She does her errands. She has her friends. But she'd rather they came over. She likes to stay close to home. Still, she laughs. A little nervous, a little watchful. But she does smile.

If you'd never known her before, you'd say she was just like that. You'd never guess she'd been another person. Before what happened... A person she dropped all at once, like a tree dropping its leaves.

Done

Did you think I'd be sorry? For what? For the way I treated you? For not understanding you?

For Godssake, grow up.

That's what I'd say, if you could somehow get the guts to pull together your dust and come back as a halfway decent ghost, and ask, "So what do you think of me now, huh? How do you feel about it all now?" I'd ask you right back, "Do they have a kindergarten over there? Nursery school? Because I don't care how old you were when you threw it all in, you've got a long eternity before you get to first grade."

I can just see you, hunched up in your little corner, thinking of how you'd stick it to us all. You could taste it, couldn't you, like saffron on your lips, like honey in your throat? You savored it, like a vintage bouquet.

Only, you were wrong. How about that? Everyone's pissed at you. If anyone goes to your grave, it's so they can spit on it.

Seriously. You lost. You blew it. Your whole plan went down the tubes. All the tears, all the obligatory lamentations, have been cried out. The sorry party's over. Now it's back to business, and you're not on the agenda. Now it's time for the feast and no one set you a place. You cast a shadow, but only for a moment. The sun's done with you, and so are we.

Hole in the Sky

He tore a hole in the sky. That's how it feels.

It'll be a beautiful, sunny day, hardly a cloud in sight, children screeching as they run about; everything as it should be. And yet there'll be this hole, right there in the blue, waiting, waiting with its steep, jagged walls, and its bottomless depths.

I try to ignore it, to focus on the blue sky, to listen to the running and the screaming, the happy fake screaming of children who need something to be scared of, who look for monsters, things they can run from, alive with their own gleeful panic. I try to hear that, and to feel the breeze, to breathe in the light, but the whole time I know it's there, that gash in the sky, and I think of him making it.

I think of him leaving.

I think of him leaving all this, and wonder, wonder despite myself, where did he go? What was so wonderful about it, what is down there, down there at the bottom, and what made it so strong, so irresistible? And I find myself turning towards it, trying to make it out, to see it clearly, and feeling, feeling despite myself, there's only one way to do that and that is to follow him, to follow him down to wherever he went.

Not Like Me

The Club

You're not like me. Not at all. Not the same class, not the same style, not the same age. We don't wear the same clothes, we don't speak the same way, we don't share the same beliefs.

We're not alike, you know. Not alike at all.

So how did we end up together? How did this one event seize us and bind us each to the other? Who exiled us, drove us from a place we never knew was blessed? Not until we found ourselves here. Here where it hurts to breathe, where simply waking is worse than nightmares used to be.

We're decent people, most of us. But there are bad ones too. It's not like it's a reward, or a punishment either.

It's what happened.

Justice doesn't figure in. Don't ever try to believe it does.

It's what happened, and here we are, each bearing its stamp, each one a member of the club. What can we do then but gather, and embrace, and sit down together to our awful meal?

Confidante

So your father killed himself, huh? That must have been tough. And you're not over it, are you? Even years later.

Of course you aren't. You can't fool me.

I wouldn't tell you this, but... well, you've been through it. It's not like it would shock you. Both my parents killed themselves. That's right. Both. My father first. He used a gun. I think it had to do with money. I don't know. I was pretty young at the time.

We lived by the river. It was one of the few nice things about the house. Until my mother drowned herself. Then it didn't seem so nice.

I keep away from rivers now.

Anyway. You see? It's not like you'll upset me. Go right ahead. Feel free to talk.

Come on, tell me. Tell me all about it.

The Beautiful Daughter

Your daughter dances so beautifully. You must be very proud of her.

They can be such a joy, children. Even the ones who don't do well. They don't have to be talented or accomplished. You love them for themselves. Just because they're there.

Though it's easy to forget, isn't it? To forget to tell them that. To let them know you love them, even if they do nothing at all. Even if they never get up on that stage.

It's hard because you do want them to do well, so you may push them, just a little, to be better. Because you love them, you know? Because you want them to shine.

And they may even act as if they want to get there too. To where it is you're pushing them. Because they want so to please you, to make you love them – as if you wouldn't anyway, how ever did they get that idea? But they did – that is, they might, and so they'd try harder, harder and harder to please you, and to make you think they liked it, when in fact it's crushing them, it's making them sick inside, sick, at just the thought of failing, of not making it to that peak, that peak where they'll find your love.

And then all at once they panic, they can't hold on any longer, and they let go, and they fall, fall before you know it, before you suspect anything's wrong, and the next thing you know you're left with nothing, not a thing, and all that love, all that love they thought they had to work for, it's pouring out, it's flooding, flooding into nowhere, with no one to catch it, no one to drink it in, just spilling away.

Lost.

She's beautiful, your daughter. I want you to know that. I just want you to look at her, to look at her and see.

28

Foreclosed

Henry!

Hey man. I wanted to touch base on the Fowler situation.

The big guy says to hold off on foreclosure. At least until after the funeral. We don't need videos all over the Web of her grieving family being put out on the street.

You know the funeral's this weekend, right? The way she did it, they'll have to go with a closed casket. You can bet the papers will splash that all over the front page with "FORECLOSED" stamped across it.

Tacky, huh? But you know journalists.

Look, I sent you a list of names. I need you to vet it for me. See who else might take a shotgun shortcut out of debt. My girls over here don't need another "Goodbye cruel world" fax. It really puts morale in the toilet, you dig?

Be a pal, would you, and get the list back to me pronto? We don't need people thinking this is a license to default.

OK, guy?

Peace. Out.

The General

When I told them to shoot the children, and the mothers too, I did not think of my daughter, safe on our terrace back home, sipping chilled wine while she studied.

She was made to be a doctor. She had always been so caring.

I had left her a gun, only because she was a woman alone. And who knew better than I what could happen to a woman alone?

Sometimes at the front we got the foreign papers, the ones that called me "the Butcher". "Lies," my men would laugh, "All lies! Let them show proof." But of course we made sure there was no proof. And when I called my daughter, I told her, "Don't believe that propaganda. They welcome us here. With flowers and parades."

Then one day a paper came with pictures – pictures of the bodies, pictures of the graves. I exploded. "How did this happen? Who let these get through?" I was too angry to think of my daughter.

But back home, she was thinking of me – of her hero father, the father who'd lied to her. The father who'd left her a gun. She laid that same paper out before her, with its awful weight of proof. Then she erased those images, and her love for me, with a single shot.

With one shot she defeated me, defeated the feared, powerful general.

Dancer

He danced with me, and I was so proud, almost as if I was twelve again, as if I'd never gone to college or had a career. It was that simple, that familiar, to lean again against his chest, and I spun away and I returned, and he moved with his old grace, hesitating here and there, but still the expert, still the one I'd trust, wherever he went, whatever he did, and we danced one dance and then another, and then the night was over, and I went back to my life, my busy, busy grown-up life, and he never said he was tired, he never said he was sad, but before the week was over, he ran a hose from his car exhaust to the driver side window, and got inside, and danced away, danced away forever; and I don't know where he went, and I don't know why he did it, but my arms are still held out, held out waiting, waiting in vain for him to return.

Something Out There

Something Out There

What would it take to make you do it?

Let's say, right off, you're not depressed. Seriously depressed. That worm eating your being, and no one can see it, and no one can cure it, and every trick you try keeps sending you back, back down that hole.

Say it's not that.

What about loss? What about losing someone you never dreamed you'd be without, and suddenly you're alone, and those eyes, that voice, that person who completed you, or made life magic, or simply understood you – that person was gone. Would you follow? Would you simply give up?

Probably not. Probably you'd get over it.

Say money then. A lot of money. What if you lost it all and ended up in debt you'd never be able to repay? What if you knew they were coming to get you, that the good times were over, that the bad times were about to begin? For good.

Would you do it then? Would you take the easy way out?

You might. You don't know. People have.

How about pain? Pain that didn't stop. Pain that made it impossible to think. Pain you knew for sure would last. Would never end.

You think you'd hold on then? Would you? How? Drugs? What if the drugs didn't work? You think you'd hang in there?

Just tough it out. That simple, huh?

You don't know. Admit it.

You simply can never know if there's something out there. Something that, one day, will be too big for you to beat.

The Rush

"You're gonna kill yourself," I said.

"But it's such a rush," he told me, "There's nothing like it."

"I get that. I do. But how many times have you almost bought it? I mean, cashed out entirely."

"More than once," he says, "More than once."

"And that's what I'm saying," I said. "You won't always be so lucky. One day - "

"One day." he says. "But it hasn't happened yet."

"Well no," I said, "no. You've got me there. It hasn't happened yet."

"Right. Look at me. I'm still alive. Completely alive."

"But that's luck," I said, "blind luck."

"Isn't it though?" he said, "Isn't it just?"

"You've got to know that one day, it'll happen."

"I do. I do know that." And he nodded.

"It'll all be done then. All that rush. All that fun."

"Absolutely." And he nodded again.

"What I'm trying to tell you -" – this was frustrating me now, that he kept missing my point – "is, you keep this up, it's not even a bet, it's a sure thing, you keep this up, and you're going to die."

And he shook his head, and he looked me up and down, and he said, "You don't get it, do you? You don't get it at all."

35

Wonderful

This reporter just left. She wanted to know how I did it. How I came so far so fast. What's so special about me, she wanted to know, that got me ahead of the pack? Wasn't it wonderful, she asked, to have so much happen all at once?

"Yes," I said, "wonderful. Simply wonderful."

Then, the moment she left, I went over to the window and threw it open. I leaned way out, looking down to the street, eight stories below, and I thought how wonderful it would be, just wonderful, to let go, and fall.

But instead I pulled back inside and I called you. I almost didn't. I was too embarrassed. Embarrassed to be ungrateful. Embarrassed by all I've got that I don't deserve. But the God's honest truth is, I don't feel like I've got a thing. I feel naked and helpless, and I have no idea what I'm doing or where I'm going.

They want to know, all of them, how I made it. But me, all I want to know is how to make it, just make it through one more day.

The Code

It is noble to die for honor. To die at the hand of an enemy is best. But if you prove unworthy to fall, then the greatest honor left to you is to die by your own hand.

You have no right, however, to cast away your own life lightly. You must do it with measure and respect. There must be incense; there must be chanting.

And pain. You must bear great pain.

Do not neglect this.

The samurai, when they had shamed themselves, would thrust the proper blade into the center of their belly and draw it slowly across to the other side while chanting their death poem. A poem they had composed.

Isn't that a fine image? Isn't that inspiring?

Except for the blood, spilling out on their knees, and the stink of the waste from their guts. What a stench. It must have somewhat spoiled the effect.

The important thing, though, is that they suffered, and they chanted, and they did it in accordance with the code.

That is what is noble, to not be left alone with your own failure, to stay one with the warriors to the last. Because you have obeyed. Because you have done what the Way demands.

Because, in the end, you died, yes. But you died by the Code.

Lucky in the End

So I bought a gun. That's easy, right? We live in America. Anyone can buy a gun. And bullets. I almost forgot those. The kid at the counter should have reminded me. But he was glued to his cell phone, chatting up some babe. He just wanted me out of there. On top of that, two minutes later, I'm back. He was so not glad to see me. Grabbed a box, threw it in a bag and rang me up.

When I got home, I moved all my stuff away from one wall, backed my easy chair up against it. One good coat of paint and no harm done. They could dump the chair.

Next I went to write a note. On my computer. But halfway through it the sucker hung. It's done that a lot lately. I could have rebooted, but come on... A simple note, for cryin' out loud.

So I decided to write it by hand. If I could find a pen. My last one had died while I was writing a check. I almost went out for another one, then I thought, "To pay a bill? Why the hell am I still paying my bills?" And I laughed. And laughed and laughed.

I hadn't done that in a long time.

Only, here I was now, without a pen.

What I finally did was, I found some lipstick. Hers. So I cleared off my kitchen table and used it to write a note. But shorter. Shorter than I'd planned.

I mean, have you ever tried writing with lipstick? It doesn't exactly encourage eloquence.

After that, I took a dump. Just because. I had to. Life goes on, right?

At least for a while.

Then I got in the chair, and I took out the gun. It had looked so simple at the store, but now it looked complicated. Scary, even. Still, soon I got up to speed - how to open it, pop the safety, all that. Until I went to load the bullets. Which wouldn't go in.

Would you believe?

The kid gave me the wrong kind.

The Number

That number was still in my book. I'd forgotten it was there. But I was thumbing through the pages, my mind somewhere else. And there it was.

I hadn't even thought of it, since... Since before. Then I knew it by heart. But since... Since then, I'd blocked it out. Scraped it from my brain cells. So this was like I'd tripped over it, and fallen flat on my face.

That's how hard it hit me. It all rushed in again, all at once. All that failure. All those regrets. Washing over me, dragging me out with the undertow. And I had nothing to cling to. Nothing at all.

You don't understand, do you? I've seen you. Even when you get slammed, even when you should be shattered, you've got that... thing? That thing you always manage to turn to.

I'm not like that. Not yet. Maybe never. I don't have that rock, that harbor inside.

But I do know how to ask for help. Now I do. So I reached for the phone. And dialed the number. Not the one in my book. The other one.

The one for people who can't do it on their own.

The woman this time was pretty good. She let me talk, then asked me questions. Gently, ever so gently. Still, I could see where she was going. I knew how bad I sounded; I could feel her talking to what she thought she heard. So I broke in. "You don't understand," I said. "I've made my choice: I want to live. I'm sure of that now."

"The thing is, I still don't know how."

The Expert

Why do people commit suicide? One might suggest a number of reasons: because they are depressed; because they are in pain; because they feel abandoned.

But such answers tell us nothing. People not only live with crushing depression, with chronic pain, but live to create, to lead, to make a name. In a word, to triumph. How many millionaires once were ruined? How many athletes overcame injuries to win?

Oh, many, myself included, have studied the subject, have compiled statistics, analyzed social norms, interviewed twins and adoptees, trying to find the fault line, the place where some split while others stay whole. But no one has found it, claim what they will.

No one knows.

I don't know. For all the years of late nights, for all the peering I've done into that darkness, I have no answer. All my work has led me nowhere.

Is that why I'm doing this? Because I'm discouraged? Because I'm weary of the struggle?

I won't try to leave you an answer. It's bad enough that the papers will call me, "One of the foremost experts on suicide..." Because the one thought I can leave you with is this: when it comes to suicide, there are no experts.